Table of Contents

Which one should I make?

Bravo Felt Mascots

Hi, we're Aranzi Aronzo.
This is the Aranzi Aronzo book of felt mascots.
Bunnies, pandas, sprites, bears, fish, bad guys, and more.

In this book are instructions on how to make felt mascots.
By reading this book you can learn to make mascots in a cinch.
But that's not all.
This book also contains the cutie vibe of felt mascots.
By simply looking at the book you can enjoy the felt mascot universe.

But you will probably have more fun making the mascots yourself.
They're all easy to make, so go make one today,
put it on your purse tomorrow, and away you go!
Everyone will say, "how cute!" (we promise)
People will be jealous and might even resent you. Be careful.

Cute felt mascots. Easy to make felt mascots.
Nice felt mascots. Crazy felt mascots.
BRAVO! FELT MASCOTS!

Basics Are Important

What do we need? How do we use them?

These are the basic materials.

Embroidery Needle
For stitching with 3-6 strands.

Colored Pencil Charcoal Pencil
For outlining your pattern. It's best to have a pencil you can easily erase, in case you make a mistake, but a simple colored pencil will do.

Scissors
For cutting out your pattern. For cutting your fabric. For cutting your yarn.

Sewing Needle
For stitching with 1-2 strands.

Glue
To stick pieces of felt and yarn on your mascot.

Fabric
We will suggest basic colors in the list of materials for each mascot, but you don't have to pay any attention. Just use the colors you want!

These colors aren't weird at all.

Cotton
To stuff the mascots' bodies and faces.

Cotton

A Thin Stick-like Object
Convenient for stuffing the narrow parts of your mascot with cotton. Bamboo skewers, toothpicks and q-tips, or anything like that in your house is good.

Embroidery Threads
There are some basic suggestions on thread color but in general, the thread color should be close to the fabric color.

With 1 strand
Knot one end of our yarn

and thread it through your sewing needle.

How To Sew

With 6 strands
With 6 strands, knot one end of 6 strands

or both ends of 3 strands

With an embroidery needle, you can either thread the needle with 6 strands and knot one end, or thread the needle with 3 strands and knot the ends together. It's the same!

Overlock
Stitching the edges of fabric is called overlock. If you tilt the needle slightly diagonal to the fabric, it will make the sewing hole much cleaner.

View from top

View from side

The French Knot Stitch
This stitch is often used for creating the eyes and nose of mascots.

Double French Knot
Pull needle through fabric and wrap thread around needle twice.

Triple French Knot
Pull needle through fabric and wrap thread around needle three times.

With thread still wrapped around the needle put needle back into fabric right next to where it came out.

Tada!

Straight Stitch (S-Stitch)
In a straight stitch you create a straight line with your thread.

Basics Are Important

> Eek!

> What's wrong?

> I can't get it right.

> You know, I have a knack for this.

The knack for making a pattern

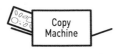

Copy Machine

OR

Photocopy your pattern off the book and cut it out.

Put a thin piece of paper on top of the pattern in the book and trace an outline, then cut it out.

If you want a pattern that will last, simply take your photocopy or traced paper and glue it onto a piece of thick paper, and then cut it out.

The knack for transferring your pattern to the fabric

Put your pattern on top of the felt. Transfer the outline onto the fabric with your charcoal or colored pencil. Use dark-colored pencils for light fabrics. Use light-colored pencils for dark fabrics.

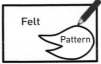

Felt

Pattern

The knack for making cute faces on your mascots

Placement of the eyes, nose and mouth should match the picture of the finished mascot. If you loosen the S-stitch of the mouth, you can make it look like it's smiling.

Loosen

Use a thin stick (e.g. a toothpick) to apply glue on the back

If you apply a little bit of glue on the back of the mouth stitch, you can keep the smile in place.

The knack for getting the legs, arms and ears looking awesome

The image at the bottom of the right-hand page is what the finished mascot looks like in actual size. Use it as a guide to place the pieces exactly where they need to go, by putting the cut-out felt flush against the image first.

Felt

Stick on

Stick on

Stick on

Stick on

Stick on

The knack for stuffing your mascots

stuff

stuff

Stuff the easy-to-insert parts using your finger or the end of a pencil.

In the narrower parts, use a thin object with a dull end and squeeze the stuffing in.

squish

squish

White Rabbit
Brown Bunny

White Rabbit and Brown Bunny
are best girl friends.
They are two of the cutest mascots
with their floppy ears, arms and legs.
They are really easy to make
but so cute.

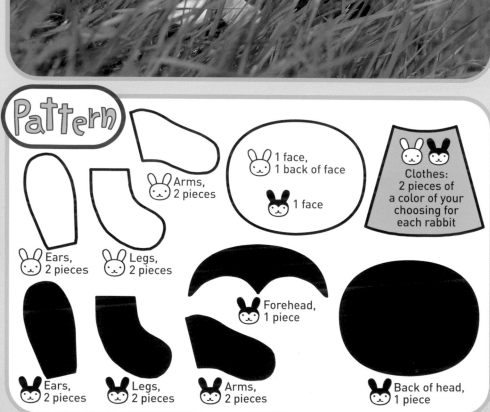

Pattern

Arms,
2 pieces

1 face,
1 back of face

1 face

Clothes:
2 pieces of
a color of your
choosing for
each rabbit

Ears,
2 pieces

Legs,
2 pieces

Forehead,
1 piece

Ears,
2 pieces

Legs,
2 pieces

Arms,
2 pieces

Back of head,
1 piece

Materials

Felt

White | Dark Brown | Any color you like for the clothes

Embroidery thread

White
Dark Brown
Color of the clothes

Cotton

1 Eyes: triple French knot
brown thread, 6 strand knot
Nose: double French knot

2 Make the mouth with a straight stitch
brown thread, 6 strand knot

3 If you loosen the straight stitch on the mouth, you can make it look like its smiling
Loosen
Completed mouth

4 Glue the forehead onto the center-top of the face

5 Stick the ears in and overlock stitch them in place
1 strand of white thread

6 Stuff with cotton and stitch shut
Cotton

7 Stick the ears in and overlock stitch them in place
1 strand of brown thread and white thread

8 Stitch forehead with brown thread
white thread
Cotton
Stuff with cotton and stitch shut

9 Using the finished image, place the arms and legs in the right place

10 Stick in the arms and legs and overlock stitch them into the clothes
Cotton
Stuff them with cotton and stitch shut
1 strand stitch

11 Sew the head onto the clothes at the neck
white thread, 1 strand

Done

7

Sprite

The spry Mr. Sprite is pretty spritely, even as a felt mascot. Make Mr. Sprite look especially spry when you craft him.

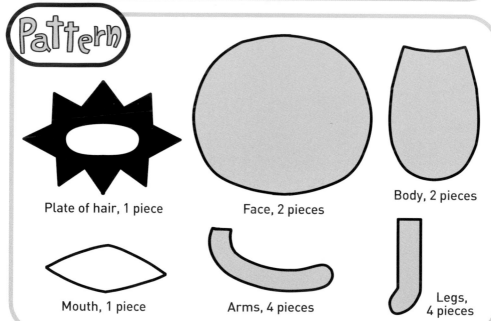

Pattern

Plate of hair, 1 piece

Face, 2 pieces

Body, 2 pieces

Mouth, 1 piece

Arms, 4 pieces

Legs, 4 pieces

Materials

Felt

Light Blue | Dark Brown | Light Yellow

Embroidery thread

Light Blue
Black
Brown

Cotton

---

1. Eyes: triple French knot
black thread, 6 strand knot
brown thread, 2 strand knot
Nose: single French knot

2. Mouth: glue the pattern onto face

3.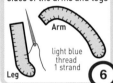
Lips: straight stitch
4 strands of light blue thread

4. Overlock stitch the face and stuff it with cotton, stitch shut
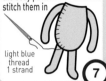
light blue thread 1 strand
Cotton

---

5. Center the plate of hair and glue it on top of the head
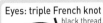
Paste
Back
Front

6. Overlock stitch the two sides of the arms and legs

Arm
light blue thread 1 strand
Leg

7. Stick the arms and legs into the body pattern and overlock stitch them in
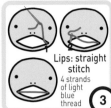
light blue thread 1 strand

8. Stuff the body and stitch shut
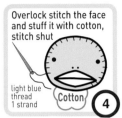
Cotton

---

9. Sew the head onto the body at the neck
light blue thread 1 strand

10. If you tweak the shape or placement of the arms and legs, you can get this

11. or even this

Done

9

Bear

This totally unserious and spaced-out-looking bear can easily change his expression with his white eyes and black pupils. Glaring, side-glancing, sleepy-eyed, surprised, etc.

 **Pattern**

 Inner ears, 2 pieces

 Outer ears, 2 pieces

Face, 2 pieces

 Whites of the eyes, 2 pieces

Arms, 2 pieces

Muzzle, 1 piece

Clothes, 2 pieces in a color of your choosing

 Legs, 2 pieces

Materials

Felt

Dark Brown | White | Any color you like for the clothes

Embroidery thread

Brown
Black
Color of the clothes

Cotton

---

1. Glue the whites of the eyes to the face

Glue the muzzle to the face

2. Eyes: triple French knot

black 6 threaded knot

3. Nose: double French knot

black 6 threaded knot

4. Mouth: straight stitch

black 6 threaded knot

1 2 3 4

5. If you loosen the straight stitch of the mouth, you can make the bear smile

6. Insert the ends of the outer ears into the head and overlock stitch them

brown thread, 1 strand

7. Stuff the face with cotton

Cotton

8. Glue the inner ears onto the outer ears

9. Position the arms and legs

10. Overlock stitch the arms and legs into the clothes and stuff it with cotton

Overlock stitch with 1 strand of thread the color of the clothes

Cotton

11. Sew the face onto the body

brown thread, 1 strand

Done

11

Panda

Panda gets upset, laughs, and is an altogether dramatic panda with an extreme personality. Black and white and simple, Panda's size can be altered, and its color-scheme changed.

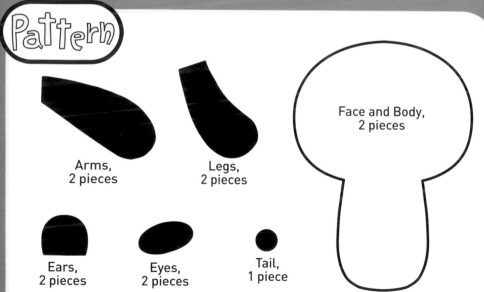

Pattern

Arms,
2 pieces

Legs,
2 pieces

Face and Body,
2 pieces

Ears,
2 pieces

Eyes,
2 pieces

Tail,
1 piece

You can alter the size of your panda by reducing/enlarging when you photocopy this image.

Felt

White | Black

Embroidery thread

White
Black

Cotton

Nose: double French knot — black thread, 6 strands

1

Mouth: straight stitch — black thread, 6 strands

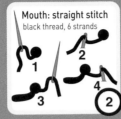

1 2 3 4

2

Glue on the eyes

3

If you loosen the straight stitch of the mouth and tilt the ends of the eyes down, Panda looks like he's smiling

4

If you stiffen the straight stitch of the mouth and tilt the ends of the eyes up, Panda looks like he's mad

5

Position the arms, legs and ears using the finished image

6

Overlock stitch the arms and legs in place

white thread 1 strand

Start

7

When you reach this point start filling the body with cotton

Cotton

Till here

8

Stick in the ears and overlock stitch them in

white thread

9

Stuff the head with cotton and sew shut

Cotton

10

Put some glue on the tail and stick it onto the butt

11

Done

Squirrel

Squirrel's face, her personality, even her clothes are all so cute. Her curly cute tail is key. So make her a cute tail, ok? And make her stripes cute too, ok? Thanks.

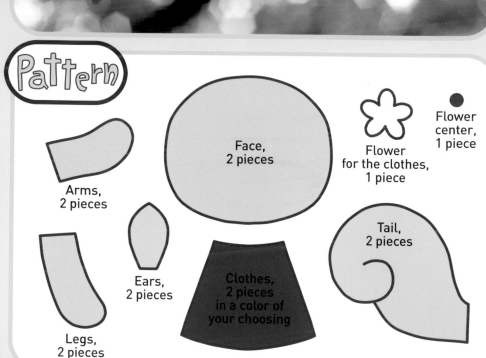

Pattern

Arms,
2 pieces

Face,
2 pieces

Flower
for the clothes,
1 piece

Flower
center,
1 piece

Ears,
2 pieces

Clothes,
2 pieces
in a color of
your choosing

Tail,
2 pieces

Legs,
2 pieces

Materials

Felt

Flesh-colored | White | Any color you like for the clothes

Embroidery thread
- Flesh-colored
- Brown
- Color of the clothes

Cotton

Colored pencil — Brown

Eyes: triple French knot
brown 6 threaded knot

brown 6 threaded knot

Nose: double French knot

1

Mouth: straight stitch
brown 6 stranded knot

1 2 3 4

Loosen the straight stitch for a smile

2

Inserting ears into face, overlock stitch them, stuff the face with cotton, and sew it up

flesh-colored thread, 1 strand   Cotton

3

Put glue on the flower and glue onto the clothes

4

Insert the arms and legs and overlock stitch them in

1 strand of thread the color of the clothes

5

Stuff with cotton and sew shut

Cotton

6

Sew the face onto the body

flesh-colored thread, 1 strand

7

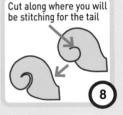

Cut along where you will be stitching for the tail

8

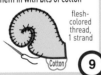

Sew the two pieces of the tail together while gradually filling them in with bits of cotton

flesh-colored thread, 1 strand

Cotton

9

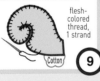

Draw stripes on the face and tail with the brown colored pencil

Front   Back

Front   Back

10

Sew the tail onto the back of the clothes

flesh-colored thread, 1 strand

Up to here

From here

11

Done

15

Fish

Fish is mature.
Perfect for mature people.
The flower patterns on that body,
the sexy lips,
the alluring gaze –
so many eye-catching features!

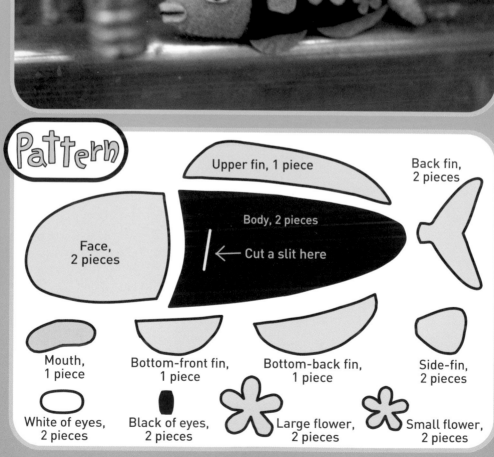

Pattern

Upper fin, 1 piece

Back fin,
2 pieces

Face,
2 pieces

Body, 2 pieces

← Cut a slit here

Mouth,
1 piece

Bottom-front fin,
1 piece

Bottom-back fin,
1 piece

Side-fin,
2 pieces

White of eyes,
2 pieces

Black of eyes,
2 pieces

Large flower,
2 pieces

Small flower,
2 pieces

Materials

Felt		
	Pink	Black
Light Blue	Dark Brown	White

Embroidery thread

Light Blue

Brown

Cotton

Eyes: glue them onto the face like this

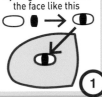

(1)

Sew the face up

1 strand of light blue thread

From here

To here

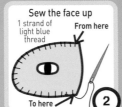

(2)

Mouth: glue it onto the face like this

One side   Other side

(3)

The lip line: straight stitch

brown thread, 4 strands

(4)

Put a slit into the body

Side   Stick the side-fin into the slit

Side → Side

Sew from the other side like you're scooping out the hole

Other side

brown thread, 1 strand

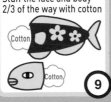

(5)

Glue the flowers onto the body

triple French knot stitch

brown thread, 6 strands

(6)

Position the fins using the image below

Reverse side

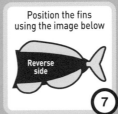

(7)

Overlock stitch them in place

To here   1 strand of brown thread

From here

(8)

Stuff the face and body 2/3 of the way with cotton

Cotton

Cotton

(9)

Push the face into the body

Combined

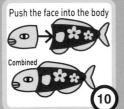

(10)

---

1 strand of brown thread

Cotton

As you continue to stuff with cotton, sew the face into the body (11)

Done

17

Monkey

He's a serious monkey.
He's from Japan.
That's why his tail is short.
He's not a chimp.
He's a monkey.
Please craft him seriously.

Pattern

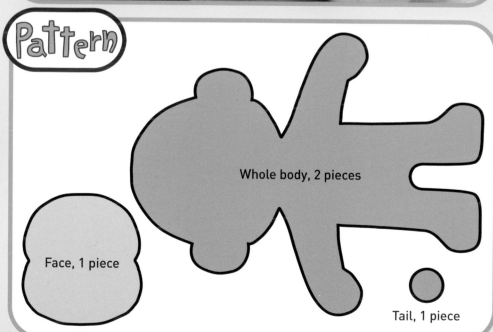

Face, 1 piece

Whole body, 2 pieces

Tail, 1 piece

Materials

Felt	Embroidery thread	

Felt

 Light Brown

Flesh-colored

Embroidery thread

Light Brown

Flesh-colored

Brown

Cotton

1

Eyes: triple French knot
brown thread, 6 strands

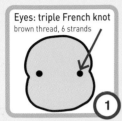

2

Forehead wrinkles:
straight stitch

brown thread,
6 strands

3

Voilà,
the forehead wrinkles

4

Nose and mouth:
straight stitch

brown
thread,
6 strands

Pierce

Pull

Pull

1

Sewing order   Pierce 2

5

3 Pull
4 Pierce
6 Pierce
5 Pull
8 Pierce
7 Pull
9 Pull
10 Pierce

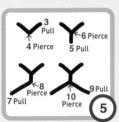

6

Voilà, the face

7

Decide placement of the face
on the head and sew in

1 strand of
flesh-
colored
thread

8

Overlock stitch the body

1 strand
of light
brown
thread

9

As you sew it up,
stuff with cotton little
by little

Cotton

10

The arms and legs are
narrow, so squeeze in
the cotton with a thin
blunt-tipped stick

Cotton   squish
squish

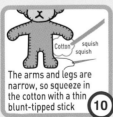

11

Put some glue on the tail
and stick it on the butt

Done

White Sheep Black Sheep

Sheep are quiet.
They are unassuming.
The felt mascots of sheep are also
unassuming. If you make them
out of fleece-like fabric,
they will look especially realistic.

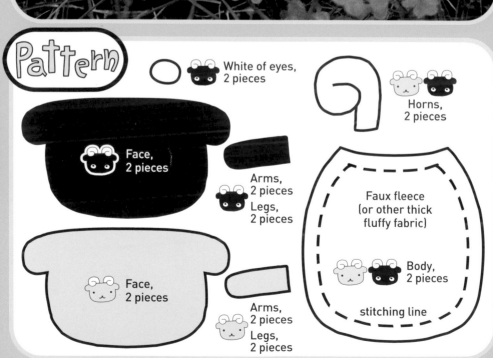

Pattern

White of eyes,
2 pieces

Horns,
2 pieces

Face,
2 pieces

Arms,
2 pieces
Legs,
2 pieces

Faux fleece
(or other thick
fluffy fabric)

Body,
2 pieces

stitching line

Face,
2 pieces

Arms,
2 pieces
Legs,
2 pieces

20

Felt

White | Flesh-colored | **Black**

Embroidery thread

Flesh-colored
Black
White

Cotton

White fleece fabric

Eyes: triple French knot

black thread, 6 stranded knot

Nose: double French knot

1

Mouth: straight stitch

black thread, 6 strands

Loosen the thread to make it look like it's smiling

2

White of eyes: glue onto face
Pupils: triple French knot

black thread, 6 strands

Make him look sulky by stitching the pupils up high

3

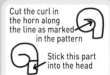

Cut the curl in the horn along the line as marked in the pattern

Stick this part into the head

Curl

4

Overlock stitch and stuff with cotton

black thread, 1 strand

Cotton

flesh-colored thread, 1 strand

5

With the backside of the fleece fabric facing out

Insert the arms and legs

Insert the legs

6

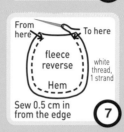

From here — To here

fleece reverse

Hem

white thread, 1 strand

Sew 0.5 cm in from the edge

7

Turn it inside-out, fill with cotton and sew shut

Cotton

white thread, 1 strand

8

Sew the head onto the body

thread the color of face, 1 strand

9

Back

10

Sew on the arms

flesh-colored thread, 1 strand

11

Done

White Cat
Striped Cat
Black Cat

Cats go meow meow.
White Cat meow, Black Cat meow,
Striped Cat meow.
There are other cats too: tabby cat,
alley cat, calico cat...
You can make your cat according to
the neighborhood kitty too you kneow.

Pattern

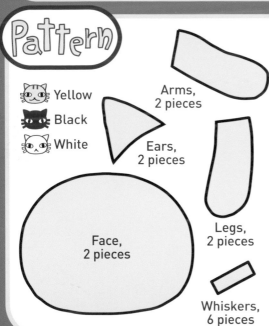

Arms,
2 pieces

🐱 Yellow

🐱 Black

🐱 White

Ears,
2 pieces

Face,
2 pieces

Legs,
2 pieces

Whiskers,
6 pieces

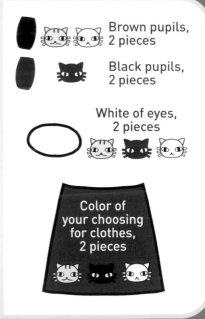

Brown pupils,
2 pieces

Black pupils,
2 pieces

White of eyes,
2 pieces

Color of
your choosing
for clothes,
2 pieces

Materials

Felt				Embroidery thread		

Felt
- Any color you like for the clothes

- Yellow
- Black
- White
- Brown

Embroidery thread
- Yellow
- White
- Black
- Brown
- Color of clothing and buttons

Cotton

Colored pencil
- Brown

---

1 — Glue on the eye whites and pupils

2 — Backstitch around the white of the eyes
brown thread, 4 strands

3 — Repeat once around the white of eyes to make them stand out on White Cat

4 — Nose: single French knot
brown thread, 6 stranded knot
black thread

5 — Straight stitch the mouth
brown thread, 6 strands
black thread

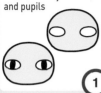

6 — Position the whiskers on the backside of the face and glue them on
Wait until the glue dries
Put glue on the end-points of the whiskers
Reverse

7 — Insert the ears to the face and overlock stitch them
face-colored thread, 1 strand
Cotton

8 — Buttons on clothing: triple French knot
6 strands, thread of any color you like

9 — Inserting arms and legs, overlock stitch them in, stuff with cotton and sew shut
Cotton
clothes-colored thread, 1 strand

10 — Sew the head onto the clothes
face-colored thread, 1 strand

11 — Draw in the stripes with your colored pencil
brown colored pencil

Done

23

Bird

Very girly, excellent figure, coquettish, but confused little bird. "I would like you to make me very pretty."

Pattern

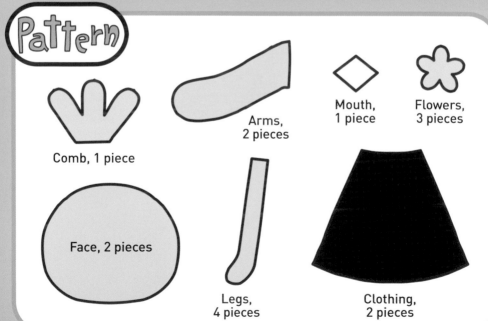

Comb, 1 piece

Arms, 2 pieces

Mouth, 1 piece

Flowers, 3 pieces

Face, 2 pieces

Legs, 4 pieces

Clothing, 2 pieces

Materials

Pink	Light Blue
Felt	Light Yellow

Embroidery thread

Pink	
Dark Yellow	
Red	
Black	

Cotton

1. Eyes: triple French knot
black thread, 6 strands

2. Mouth: glue onto face

3. Lip line: straight stitch
1   2
dark yellow thread, 4 strands

4. Insert the comb onto the head and overlock stitch
pink thread, 1 strand

5. Stuff the head with cotton and sew shut
Cotton

6. Position the flowers onto the dress

7. Sew in the flowers with a French knot stitch
red thread, 6 stranded triple knot

8. Put two leg pieces together and sew up the sides
pink thread, 1 strand

9. Inserting arms and legs, overlock stitch in, stuff with cotton and sew shut
red thread, 1 strand

10. Sew head onto body
pink thread, 1 strand

11. You can give Bird different poses by positioning the arms and legs differently

Done

Frog

(Mr. Tad and Mr. Pole included)

Bold at home but timid outside,
that's Froggie.
Mr. Tad is sprouting limbs.
Mr. Pole is younger than Mr. Tad.
Make all three, line 'em up,
and feel the pond!

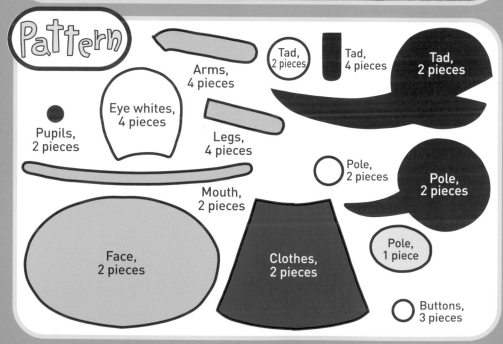

Pattern

Arms,
4 pieces

Tad,
2 pieces

Tad,
4 pieces

Tad,
2 pieces

Eye whites,
4 pieces

Pupils,
2 pieces

Legs,
4 pieces

Pole,
2 pieces

Pole,
2 pieces

Mouth,
2 pieces

Pole,
1 piece

Face,
2 pieces

Clothes,
2 pieces

Buttons,
3 pieces

Light Green	Green	White
Light Yellow	Black	Light Blue

Felt

Embroidery thread

Light Green
Green
Black
White

Cotton

---

1. Mouth: put the two pieces and sew them up together

light green thread, 1 strand

2. Position the mouth on one of the face pieces

Front
Back

Sew in the mouth from the back, scooping so the seam doesn't show in front.

3. Eyes: glue onto the eye whites

white thread, 1 strand

Overlock stitch the eyes and stuff them with cotton

Cotton

4. Insert the eyes, overlock stitch them, stuff the face with cotton and sew it up

light green thread, 1 strand

Cotton

5. Put together the two pieces of arms and legs and overlock stitch them

Arm
Leg

light green thread, 1 strand

6. Insert the arms and legs and overlock stitch them while stuffing the body with cotton

Glue on the buttons

Cotton

green thread, 1 strand

7. Sew the face onto the body

light green thread, 1 strand

8. Eye whites: glue on
Pupils: triple French knot

black thread, 6 strands

9. Insert the arms and legs, overlock stitch, stuff with cotton and sew shut

Cotton

black thread, 1 strand

10. Insert the fin and overlock stitch it in, stuff with cotton and sew shut

black thread, 1 strand

Cotton

11. Fin-lines: straight stitch

black thread, 6 strand

Done

Lizard

What a sweet Lizard,
with her bashful little smile.
The key here is to make her look calm.
You should be relaxed when
you make her.

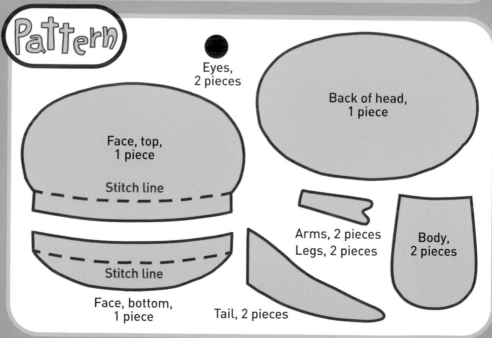

Pattern

Eyes,
2 pieces

Back of head,
1 piece

Face, top,
1 piece

Stitch line

Arms, 2 pieces
Legs, 2 pieces

Body,
2 pieces

Stitch line

Face, bottom,
1 piece

Tail, 2 pieces

Felt

| Green | Black |

Embroidery thread

Green

Cotton

Dark Green
Colored pencil

---

1. Reverse the bottom part of the face and overlay on the top, lining up the seams

Overlay

Seam

2. They won't line up perfectly—sew along the seam while stretching the stitch a little

green thread, 2 strands

3. Reverse

Margin

Fold up the leftover margin

4. The other side should look like it's smiling at the seam

Front

---

5. Eyes: glue onto the face

6. Overlock stitch the face and back of the head and stuff with cotton

green thread, 2 strands

Cotton

7. Insert the arms and legs, overlock stitch the body, stuff with cotton and sew shut

Cotton

green thread, 1 strand

8. Sew the head onto the body

green thread, 1 strand

---

9. Overlock stitch and stuff with cotton

green thread, 1 strand

Cotton

Tail

squish squish Squeeze in the cotton with a thin object

10. Sew the tail onto the backside

green thread, 1 strand

11. Make the mouth stand out by drawing in a line on the seam with a dark green colored pencil

Done

Bad Guy

The Bad Guy does bad things.
His wire arms and legs look pretty bad.
(Caution: they poke.)
His smile is so creepy.
(Caution: putting him on your purse
could get fingers pointed at your back.)

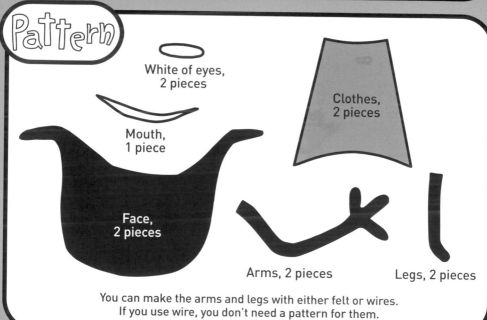

Pattern

White of eyes,
2 pieces

Mouth,
1 piece

Clothes,
2 pieces

Face,
2 pieces

Arms, 2 pieces

Legs, 2 pieces

You can make the arms and legs with either felt or wires.
If you use wire, you don't need a pattern for them.

	Embroidery thread	Pliers	
Black	Black ▬▬	If you're using wires	**Cotton**
	Grey ▬▬	**Wire**	
Felt Grey White	**Rubber bands** If you're using wires: 4 of them	Wire with black plastic coating or just plain wire is fine	

1 Glue on the eyes to the face
Glue on the mouth

2 Eyes: triple French knot
black thread, 6 strands

3 Overlock stitch the face, stuff with cotton and sew shut
black thread, 1 strand
Cotton

4 **Arms and legs, with wire**
Arms ▬▬ 15cm
Fingers ▬ 3cm, 2pieces
Legs ▬▬ 9cm
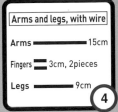

5 Wrap the arm wire ends around the finger wire and close them with pliers
Arm   Finger
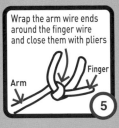

6 Position the arms and legs

7 Wrap rubber bands right behind where the arms and legs will stick out, so they don't move back and forth
Rubber bands

8 Overlock stitch, stuff with cotton, and sew shut
grey thread, 1 strand
Cotton

9 **Arms and legs, with felt**
Position the arms and legs

10 Insert the arms and legs, overlock stitch the body, stuff with cotton and sew shut
grey thread, 1 strand
Cotton

11 Sew the head onto the body
black thread, 1 strand

Done

Liar

With his upturned mouth,
and shrewd eyes,
he lies, the Liar.
With his legs side by side,
and his arms on either side of his body,
he's proud of being surreal.

Pattern

Face,
2 pieces

Eyes,
2 pieces

Arms,
2 pieces

Clothes,
2 pieces

Legs,
2 pieces

Felt

Yellow | [black square] | White

Embroidery thread

Black
Yellow
Red

Cotton

1. Eye whites: glue them on

2. Eyes: triple French knot
black thread, 6 strands

3. With a slight change in his eyes, the Liar can make all kinds of expressions

4. Overlock stitch the face
yellow thread, 1 strand

5. With a non-pointy stick, stuff the face with cotton into the corners of the face, then stitch shut
Cotton squish squish

6. Cut slits into the clothes

7. Insert the arms

8. Sew on the arms from the reverse side so you can't see the thread from the front
red thread, 1 strand

9. Insert the legs and overlock stitch the body
red thread, 1 strand

10. Stuff with cotton and sew shut
Cotton

11. Sew the head onto the body
yellow thread, 1 strand

Done

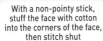

33

Alien

He came from space on a UFO.
Even after becoming a felt mascot,
he's still not that cute.
That's precisely his charm.

Pattern

Ears,
2 pieces

Mouth,
1 piece

Face,
2 pieces

Arms,
2 pieces

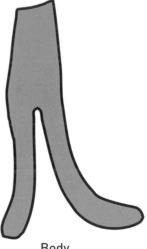

Body,
2 pieces

 **Materials**

Felt

White | Grey

Embroidery thread

Grey
Maroon

Cotton

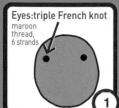
Eyes: triple French knot
maroon thread, 6 strands

1

Nose: double French knot
maroon thread, 2 strands

Mouth: glue onto face

2

If you glue the mouth on upside down, it's a smiling alien!

3

Insert the ears and overlock stitch them in
grey thread, 1 strand

4

Stuff with cotton and sew shut

Cotton

5

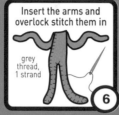
Insert the arms and overlock stitch them in
grey thread, 1 strand

6

Stuff cotton into the torso and stitch shut
Cotton
TORSO
Don't stuff the legs with cotton

7

Sew the head onto the body
grey thread, 1 strand

8

Done

35

Mechani-Panda

Face

Top and bottom, 2 pieces

Front and back, 2 pieces

Sides, 2 pieces

Stomach-door, 1 piece

Torso

Top and bottom, 2 pieces

Sides, 2 pieces

Front and back, 2 pieces

Arms

Sides, 8 pieces

Ends, 4 pieces

Legs

Sides, 8 pieces

Top and bottom, 4 pieces

Mouth, 1 piece

Eyes, 2 pieces

Tail, 1 piece

Felt

White | Black | Grey

Embroidery thread

White
Black
Grey

Cotton

1

Glue on the mouth and eyes onto the front of the face
Nose: triple French knot

Nose:
black thread, 6 strands

2

Triple French knot the ears onto the top piece of the head

Ears:
black thread, 12 strands

3

Sew all 6 sides of the head together

Back
Top
Side
Front
Side
Bottom

white thread, 1 strand

4

Stuff with cotton and sew shut

Cotton

5

Sew all 6 sides of the torso together

Back
Top
Side
Front
Side
Bottom

white thread, 1 strand

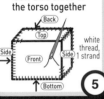

6

Stuff with cotton and sew shut

Cotton

7

Buttons on the stomach-door: triple French knot

Buttons: grey thread, 6 strands

Glue the stomach-door onto the torso front.

8

Sew the 6 sides of the arms and legs together

Cotton

black thread, 1 strand

Stuff with cotton and sew shut

9

Sew on the arms to the sides of the torso

black thread, 1 strand

10

Sew on the legs to the bottom of the torso

black thread, 1 strand

11

Sew the head onto the torso

white thread, 1 strand

Glue on the tail to the back

Back

Done

Pinkie

Pinkie.
Pinkie is Pink.
Pinkie loves Pink.
Make her with cute Pink felt.
You have to make her Pink.

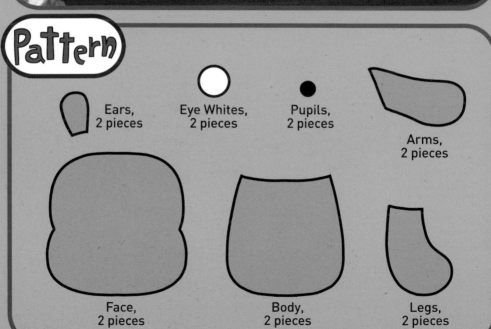

Pattern

Ears,
2 pieces

Eye Whites,
2 pieces

Pupils,
2 pieces

Arms,
2 pieces

Face,
2 pieces

Body,
2 pieces

Legs,
2 pieces

Materials

Felt

Pink | White | Black

Embroidery thread

Pink
Black

Cotton

---

1 Glue on the eye whites

2 Glue on the pupils

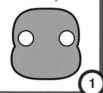

Give Pinkie the look you want

3 Eyelashes: straight stitch

black thread, 6 strands

4 Nose: double French knot

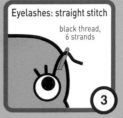

black thread, 6 strands

---

5 Straight stitch the mouth

black thread, 6 strands

1 2 3 4

6 The mouth should be big and smiley

7 Insert the ears and overlock stitch them in

pink thread, 1 strand

8 Stuff with cotton and sew shut

Cotton

---

9 Position the arms and legs

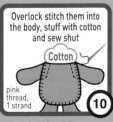

10 Overlock stitch them into the body, stuff with cotton and sew shut

Cotton

pink thread, 1 strand

11 Sew the head onto the body

pink thread, 1 strand

Done

Kidnapper

Kidnapper's job is to steal kids.
That white bag is his work bag.
Kidnapper is very trim,
so stuffing him with cotton
might be hard,
but neat and trim he must be.

**Pattern**

Hat top,
2 pieces

**Hands,
2 pieces**

Face,
2 pieces

Hat bottom,
1 piece

Body,
2 pieces

Work bag,
1 piece

Materials

Felt

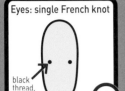 Flesh-colored | Black | White

Embroidery thread

 Flesh-colored
Black

 Cotton

1 — Eyes: single French knot
black thread, 6 strands

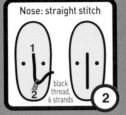
2 — Nose: straight stitch
black thread, 6 strands

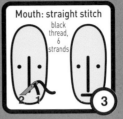
3 — Mouth: straight stitch
black thread, 6 strands

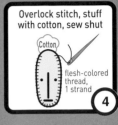
4 — Overlock stitch, stuff with cotton, sew shut
flesh-colored thread, 1 strand

5 — Insert the hands and overlock stitch the body
black thread, 6 strands

6 — Using a thin object, stuff the body with cotton. Sew shut
squish squish cotton

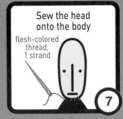
7 — Sew the head onto the body
flesh-colored thread, 1 strand

8 — Place the two sides of the hat together and sew along the top seam
black thread, 1 strand. Don't sew here

9 — Sew the bottom of the hat onto the edge of the top of the hat
black thread, 1 strand. Sew around

10 — Put the hat onto the head

11 — Make Kidnapper hold his white work bag. Glue the bag onto the inside of his hand

Done

Terry the Terrier

Terry is a wire-haired Fox Terrier.
Because he's a terrier, we call him Terry.
His real name is Terrible, which sounds
real strong and cool,
but he's not really strong at all.
Terry works for Aranzi Aronzo.
His little beady eyes are so cute.

Pattern

Face,
2 pieces

Body,
2 pieces

Ears,
2 pieces

Tail,
1 piece

 **Materials**

Felt

White

Light Brown

Embroidery thread

White

Black

Cotton

Black **Colored pencil**

Eyes: straight stitch

black thread, 6 strands

1

Nose: triple French knot

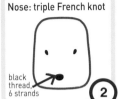

black thread, 6 strands

2

Overlock stitch the face

white thread, 1 strand

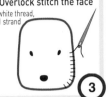

3

Stuff with cotton and sew shut

Cotton

4

Glue the ears onto the face

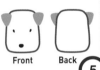

Front   Back

5

Insert the tail and overlock stitch the body

white thread, 1 strand

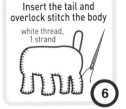

6

The legs are narrow, so use a thin object to push in the cotton as you stitch

squish squish Cotton

7

Sew shut

Cotton

8

Sew the face onto the body

white thread, 1 strand

9

Using the black colored pencil, make his back hair black

10

Other little dogs

Black   White

Fade-o   Terrie

11

Done

43

You Can Do This

How to put on an appliqué Ex: A White Rabbit tote

1 Cut the pattern

2 Give it eyes, a nose and a mouth

3 Position the felt pieces on the bag

4 Glue on the pieces with the arms, legs and ears inserted behind the dress

Use thread the same color as the felt, 1 strand

5 Sew around the edges

Done

How to make a felt stuffed toy Ex: A Giant Panda stuffed toy

Copy machine

1 With a copy machine, make a copy of the pattern that's 200-300% the original size (or whatever size you want)

2 Cut out the pieces in felt, make the eyes, nose and mouth and then glue them on

3 Sew together the two sides of the arms, legs and ears and stuff them with cotton

arms

legs

ears

Cotton

4 Insert the arms, legs and ears into the body and overlock stitch it

Done

How to make a felt mini-accessory Ex: Bear hair tie

Copy machine

1 With a copy machine, make a copy of the pattern that's 50% the original size (or whatever size you want)

Use thread that's the same color as the color of the felt, 1 strand

Done

Back

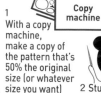

Cotton

2 Stuff with cotton and sew

3 Sew on a hair band to the back of the head

How to make a keychain Ex: Rabbit

On the very top of the back head, sew in a piece of string.

Back

swing swing

Done

How to make a keychain Ex: A Liar keychain

1 On the very top of the head, sew in a piece of string, any kind of string you want in any color you want

2 Tie up the ends of the string and make it any length you want

Use thread the same color as the felt to sew in the string, 1 strand

3 Tie it onto your bag

swing swing

Done

You Can Do That

Hair Ties

Hair Pins

Using the things you craft is fun

It's cute on bibs, but you have to be prepared to get drool on it

Sheep appliqués on your mittens make them seem warmer

A little appliqué for your little coin purse

A hanging mascot goes well on your cotton tote

Best not to use the mascots as bookmarks since it looks painful

Mr. Giant Felt Panda
and Mr. Mini Felt Panda

You can make really cute t-shirts with them too — simplicity is key here (overachievers are scary)

If you make too many, you can always give them away as presents

Let's Make Cute Stuff by Aranzi Aronzo!

Fun Dolls

Aranzi Fun Dolls

978-1-932234-79-4, 80 pages,
8.5 x 10 inches, $14.95/$21.00

Aranzi Fun Dolls introduces a new band of
characters and reintroduces old friends
in new poses, all designed to be crafted in larger
huggable versions. Full of the same easy-to-follow
patterns and instructions you've come to love
and expect from the Aranzi Aranzo craft books.

ARANZI MACHINE

What happens when the quirk critters
created by Aranzi Aronzo get together
and gallivant about town?
Aranzi Machine Gun!
Discover the world your favorite
crafty characters inhabit;
follow their adventures;
and enjoy every whimsical moment.
Plus, each volume features new
crafts presented by Miss Appliqué.

Miss Appliqué

About the Characters

White Rabbit
Carefree
Wants only to play
and eat
Not good with her
fingers

Brown Bunny
White Rabbit's friend
Cool
Good at crafts

PROFILE

ARANZI ARONZO

Aranzi Aronzo is a company that "makes what it feels like the way it feels like and then sells the stuff." Established in 1991 in Osaka. Kinuyo Saito and Yoko Yomura team. Other than original miscellany, Aranzi Aronzo also makes picture books and exhibits. Other books include *The Bad Book, Aranzi Machine Gun, Cute Dolls* and *Fun Dolls.*

http://www.vertical-inc.com/aranzi_aronzo
http://www.aranziaronzo.com

Translation — Anne Ishii

Copyright © 2007 by Aranzi Aronzo

All rights reserved.

Published by Vertical, Inc., New York.

Originally published in Japanese as *Usagi no Chiisai Tomodachi* by Kadokawa Shoten, Tokyo, 2002.

ISBN 1-932234-68-3/978-1-932234-68-8

Manufactured in Singapore

First Edition

Fourth Printing

Vertical, Inc.
www.vertical-inc.com